RABINDRA RACHANAVALI

The Trial

Autumn-Festival

Rabindranath Tagore

Rupa & Co

Concept & Typeset coypyright © Rupa & Co 2002

Published 2002 by

Rupa • Co

7/16, Ansari Road, Daryaganj
New Delhi 110 002

Sales Centres:
Allahabad Bangalore Chandigarh Chennai
Dehradun Hyderabad Jaipur Kathmandu
Kolkata Ludhiana Mumbai Pune

Design & Typeset by
Arrt Creations
45 Nehru Apts, Kalkaji
New Delhi 110 019

Printed in India by
Gopsons Papers Ltd.,
A-14 Sector 60
Noida 201 301

page ii: Rabindranath Tagore with wife Mrinalini Devi in 1883.
page vi: Unsigned. No date. Ink and poster colour on paper.
32.5 x 21.2 cm

Contents

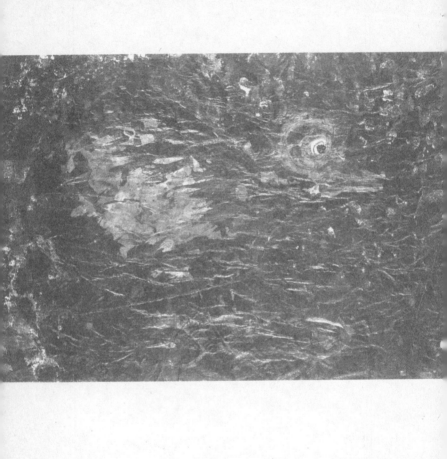

The Trial

ACT I

KHIRI *the maid servant.*

KHIRI. Some people have the means to be good in gorgeous comfort, and others like us groan under the burden of their goodness. Their charity grows fat in their easy chairs, while we carry out their mission with the sweat of our brows. They reap undying fame and we early death.

[*A voice from without: Khiri! Khiri!*]

KHIRI. There she calls! No time for poor me even to nurse my grievance!

[*Enters Rani* KALYANI.]

KALYANI. Sulky as usual!

KHIRI. That proves I am made of flesh and blood.

KALYANI. What is your latest grievance?

KHIRI. That I made a wrong choice when I chose you
for my mistress. Why should I come to a Rani's
house, if I must serve a whole world of ragged
riffraffs, cook for a needy neighbourhood bred
in dirt, and wear out my fingers washing their
dishes? And all this with nobody to help me!

KALYANI. Help you could have enough if your tongue
did not sting out all the servants I brought to
my house.

KHIRI. You are right. I have a sensitive mind, and cannot
bear the least wrong around me. This fastidious
delicacy of mine dooms me to solitude. The

servants you had were pure-blooded robbers,
blessed with a dangerously innocent look.

KALYANI. And what about yourself?

KHIRI. Holy Mother! I never claim to be an exception.
I freely take all that I can lay my hands on. Yet
I have but a single pair of them. The Creator
made these to grab and to hold; therefore if
you multiply hands about you, you divide your
possessions.

KALYANI. But your solitude seems to be bursting with
a crowd of nephews and nieces and a
miscellaneous brood of cousins. Hasn't each of
them a pair of hands for their share? You anger
me and yet make me laugh.

KHIRI. If only you laughed less and got angered more,
possibly you could have changed my nature.

KALYANI. Your nature change! Not even when you are dead.

KHIRI. This is encouragingly true. It makes me hope that death will be cautious about claiming me. There! look at that lazy crowd waiting at your gate. Some of them have the story of a sick husband, who obligingly never dies, and some of an uncle, whose death remains for ever fresh with its endless claim to funeral rites. They bring their bags full of lies, to exchange them for solid silver. I never cease to wonder how certain people can have a special relish for being cheated.

KALYANI. The poor cheat because wealth is often meaner than poverty. However, tell me why, last evening, when I fed the poor, sweets were scarce and also milk.

KHIRI. Very likely the pastryman and the milk-vendor
like to give you a fair chance to be cheated.

[*Enter neighbouring* WOMEN.]

WOMEN [*they shout*]. Long live Rani Kalyani!

KHIRI. Listen to that! If their stomachs had missed
their fill of good fare yesterday, their lungs
would show it this morning.

KALYANI. Who is that girl with you, Piari? I never saw
her before.

SECOND WOMAN. It is the new bride come to our house.
I have brought her for your blessing.

KHIRI. It is easy to guess what you mean by blessing.

KALYANI. She has a sweet face.

SECOND WOMAN. But not a particle of jewellery has she
brought from her father's house.

KHIRI. 'They are all safely stored in your own chest,'

whisper those who are in the secret.

KALYANI. Come with me into my room.

[KALYANI *goes with the* WOMAN *and the bride.*]

FIRST WOMAN. The uncommon cheek of that woman.

KHIRI. It is tiresomely common.

THIRD WOMAN. But this surpasses anything that we know.

KHIRI. Because it benefits somebody else but you.

THIRD WOMAN. Your wit makes our sides burst with laughter.

FIRST WOMAN. Whatever we may say, our Rani has the biggest heart in the world.

KHIRI. In other words, she is the biggest fool under the Sun.

FOURTH WOMAN. That is true. You remember how blind Andi was loaded with money, merely for fun, it seemed to me.

THIRD WOMAN. And that old witch of a potter woman took away from her a real woolen rug as a reward for her facility in weeping.

FOURTH WOMAN. There is no harm in charity, but must it be foolish?

FIRST WOMAN. But she has such a sweet nature.

KHIRI. A great deal of one's sweetness belongs to one's pocket.

FOURTH WOMAN. What I object to in her is her familiarity with vulgar people.

THIRD WOMAN. She could easily have a better companion, to say the least, than Kedar's mother.

FOURTH WOMAN. It is simply courting the applause of the vulgar.

KHIRI. Such is the way of the world. It is all give and

take. She supplies food to our mouths, to gather back praise from them. She gets the best of the bargain. For food is vulgar, but praise is for the great.

FOURTH WOMAN. There they, come back from the Rani's room, that woman with the bride.

FIRST WOMAN. Show us what you have got.

SECOND WOMAN. Nothing but a pair of bracelets.

THIRD WOMAN. It sounds like a practical joke.

FOURTH WOMAN. You remember Piari got for her newly married daughter a gold chain besides a pair of earrings.

SECOND WOMAN. Pity is not for the poor, but fortunate are they who have the reputation for it.

FOURTH WOMAN. The generosity of the rich is a mere hobby, it is only to please themselves.

KHIRI. If only Lakshmi, the Goddess of Luck, were

kind to me, I would show how to be kind in proper style.

SECOND WOMAN. We pray that your wish may be fulfilled.

FIRST WOMAN. Stop your chatter! I hear the Rani's footsteps!

FOURTH WOMAN [*loudly*]. Our Rani is an angel of mercy.

THIRD WOMAN. Wealth has been blessed by the touch of her hands.

[*Enters* KALYANI.]

KALYANI. What are you all so busy talking about?

KHIRI. They have been furiously ploughing the ground of your good fame, harrowing, hoeing and raking, weeding out every green thing that bore flowers.

KALYANI. Before you go home remember that if gifts had to flow parallel with expectations they would have run dry and disappeared from the world within a few days of creation.

[*She leaves the room.*]

FOURTH WOMAN. Isn't that spiteful? She must have been eavesdropping.

KHIRI. No need for that. She is old enough to know by this time that the praise that grows to excess before her face is generally pruned thin behind her back.

FOURTH WOMAN. Really, you people ought to control your tongues.

THIRD WOMAN. If only you can do it, it won't matter much if the rest of us fail.

KHIRI. Enough for the day's work of detraction. Now

you can go home with eased hearts and try to forget the smart of receiving favours. [*The women go.—she calls*] Kini, Bini, Kashi!

[*The girls come.*]

KASHI. Yes, Granny.

KINI and BINI. Yes, aunt.

KHIRI. Come and take your meal.

GIRLS. We are not hungry.

KHIRI. For eating hunger is not essential, but opportunity is. You will find some milk in the cupboard and some sweets.

KASHI. You are doing nothing but eat all day. Appetite has its limits.

KHIRI. But good things are immensely more limited. Bini, why don't I see the silver comb you had in your hair?

BINI. Poor Khetu's girl—

KHIRI. I understand. Benevolence! The plague is in the air in this house! It is fatal for a girl of your circumstances. Our Rani indulges in wasting her means only to prove that they can never be exhausted. But for you to give is to lose for ever, do you not see the difference? Now then, off to bed. [*They go.*]

[*Enters* KALYANI.]

KHIRI. Life has become a burden to me, Rani.

KALYANI. You seem to bear it with wonderful ease.

KHIRI. I swear by your feet, I am serious. I have news from home, that my aunt, my father's youngest sister, is on her death-bed.

KALYANI. A year is hardly past since I paid you the funeral expenses of this very same aunt, the youngest one.

KHIRI. What a pity! But you seem to have a keen
memory only about my poor aunts.

KALYANI. Does it choke you to ask from me? Must you
lie?

KHIRI. Lies are necessary to give dignity to begging.
Truth would be monotonous and mean.

KALYANI. But, have I ever denied you, when you asked?

KHIRI. To neglect our weapons, when not needed, is
the sure way to miss them in the time of need.
But I must tell you that you encourage lies by
believing them.

KALYANI. They will fail this time.

KHIRI. I shall not despair about my next chance. Till
then, my father's youngest sister shall never be
mentioned again.

[KALYANI *goes out laughing.*]

Mother Goddess of Luck, your favourite bird,

the owl, must have daily carried you to this house. Could it by mistake alight on my shoulder, I would feed it with choice morsels of mice flesh till it became languid and lay at my door.

[*Enters Goddess* LAKSHMI.]

KHIRI. Visitors again!

LAKSHMI. I am willing to leave, if I am not wanted.

KHIRI. I must not be rash. That seems to be a regular crown on your head. And yet you don't look ridiculous with it as a real queen would do. Tell me who you are.

LAKSHMI. I am Lakshmi.

KHIRI. Not from the stage?

LAKSHMI. No, from my heaven.

KHIRI. You must be tired. Do take your seat, and do

not be in a hurry to leave. I know full well you have no mercy for those who have brains. It is, I suppose, because the clever ones need never die of starvation and only fools need your special favour.

LAKSHMI. Are you not ashamed to make your living by cheating your mistress?

KHIRI. It is because you are perverse in your choice that those who have minds live upon those who have money.

LAKSHMI. Intellect I never despise, only the crooked minds I avoid.

KHIRI. The intellect, which is too straight, is only another name for stupidity! But if you promise me your favour, I give you my solemn word that henceforth my dullness will delight your heart. I shall be content to remain a perfect bore shunned by all intelligent people.

LAKSHMI. Do you think you will ever be able to spend a farthing in charity?

KHIRI. With pleasure. For when charity grazes only at the fringe of one's surplus, it adds to the beauty of the view—and it can also be made paying by good management. Only change our mutual position, and you will find the Rani developing a marvellous talent for devising means to get what is not her own. On the other hand, I shall become perfectly silly in swallowing lies and parting with my possessions, and my temper will grow as insipid as that of an egregious saint.

LAKSHMI. Your prayer is granted. I make you a Rani. The world will forget that you ever were a servant unless you yourself help it to remember.

ACT II

KHIRI *the Queen.*

KHIRI. Where is Kashi?

KASHI. Here I am.

KHIRI. Where are your four attendants?

KASHI. It is a perfect misery to be dogged by servants
day and night.

KHIRI. Should the elephant ever complain of the weight
of its tusks? Malati!

MALATI. Yes, Your Highness!

KHIRI. Teach this girl why she must be followed by
attendants.

MALATI. Remember that you are a Rani's grand-
daughter. In the Nawab's house, where I used
to serve, the Begum had a litter of pet

mongooses; each of them had four maids for their attendants, and sepoys besides.

KHIRI. Kashi, do you hear?

ATTENDANT. Moti of our neighbourhood craves audience.

KHIRI. Malati!

MALATI. Yes, Your Highness!

KHIRI. What is the form of salutation expected from visitors in your Begum's house?

MALATI. They have to walk forward, salaaming by touching the earth at each step, and then retire walking backward, salaaming again.

KHIRI. Let Moti come before me in proper style.

[MALATI *brings in* MOTI.]

MALATI. Bend your head low. Touch the floor, and then touch the tip of your nose. Once again— not so fast—step properly.

MOTI. Ah my poor back! How it aches!

MALATI. Take dust on the tip of your nose three times.

MOTI. I am rheumatic.

MALATI. Once again.

MOTI. Long live Rani Mother. Today, being the eleventh day of the moon, is for fasting and for almsgiving.

KHIRI. Your Rani Mother can ascertain the phases of the moon even without your help, if she finds it profitable.

MOTI. Let me receive alms from our Rani and take leave singing her praises.

KHIRI. The first part of your prayer I prefer to ignore; the rest I graciously grant. You may leave immediately singing my praises. Malati!

MALATI. Yes, Your Highness!

KHIRI. Let this woman take her leave in proper style.

MOTI. Then I go.

MALATI. Not so easily. Bend your head down. Take up
the dust of the floor on the tip of your nose.
Once again. Once more.

[MOTI *goes.*]

KHIRI. Bini, what happened to the ring you had on
your forefinger? Has it been stolen?

BINI. Not stolen.

KHIRI. Then lost?

BINI. Not lost.

KHIRI. Then someone has cheated you of it?

BINI. No.

KHIRI. You must admit that a thing either remains, or
is stolen, or lost, or. . . .

BINI. I have given it away.

KHIRI. Which plainly means that someone has cheated
you of it. Tell me, who has it?

BINI. Mallika. She is the poorest of all your servants, with her children starving. I have such a heap of rings, I thought. . .

KHIRI. Listen to her! Only those of moderate means earn fame by spending in charity, while the rich in doing it earn ingratitude. Charity has no merit for those who possess too much. Malati!

MALATI. Yes, Your Highness.

KHIRI. Mallika must be dismissed at once.

MALATI. She shall be driven away.

KHIRI. But not with the ring on her. What music is that outside my palace?

AN ATTENDANT. A marriage procession.

KHIRI. A marriage procession in front of the Rani's house! Suppose I happen to object, what is there to prevent me? Malati!

MALATI. Yes, Your Highness!

KHIRI. What do they do in a Nawab's house in such a case?

MALATI. The bridegroom is taken to the prison, and, for three days and nights two amateur flute players practice their scales at each of his ears, and then he is hanged if he survives.

KHIRI. Ask my guards to give everyone of the party ten strokes with a shoe.

FIRST ATTENDANT. Only ten strokes! It almost sounds like a caress.

SECOND ATTENDANT. They ought to rejoice at this happy ending.

THIRD ATTENDANT. Our Rani has the gift of humour, for which God be praised.

[Enters a MAID.]

MAID. My pay has been in arrears for the last nine months. To slave and yet to borrow money to feed oneself is not to my taste. Either pay up my wages or allow me leave and go home.

KHIRI. To pay up your wages is tolerably good, but it saves a lot of trouble to allow you to leave. Malati!

MALATI. Yes, Your Highness.

KHIRI. What is your advice?

MALATI. Let her be fined at least a hundred rupees.

KHIRI. As she is poor I remit fifty rupees out of her fine.

FIRST ATTENDANT. Rani, you are kind.

SECOND ATTENDANT. How lucky for her to get fifty rupees for nothing.

THIRD ATTENDANT. You can as well count it nine hundred and fifty rupees out of a thousand.

FOURTH ATTENDANT. How few are there whose charity
can be such a drain.

KHIRI. You do make me blush. [*To the* MAID] Now you
may go away with proper ceremony and finish
the rest of your weeping at leisure outside my
palace.

[MALATI *takes away the* MAID *making her walk
backwards with salaams.*]

[*Re-enters* MALATI.]

MALATI. Rani Kalyani is at your door.

KHIRI. Has she come riding on her elephant?

MALATI. No, walking. She is dusty all over.

KHIRI. Must I admit her in?

FIRST ATTENDANT. She should sit at a proper distance.

SECOND ATTENDANT. Let her stand behind your back.

THIRD ATTENDANT. She can be dismissed by saying that.
Your Highness is tired.

KHIRI. Malati!

MALATI. Yes, Your Highness!

KHIRI. Advise me what to do.

MALATI. Let all other seats be removed but your own.

KHIRI. You are clever. Let my hundred and twenty slave girls stand in a row outside that door. Sashi, hold the state umbrella over my head. Malati!

MALATI. Yes, Your Highness!

KHIRI. Is it all right?

MALATI. Perfect! like a picture!

KHIRI. Bring her into my presence.

[MALATI *goes out and returns with* KALYANI.]

KALYANI. Are you well?

KHIRI. My desire is to keep well, but the rest of the world tries its best to wreck me.

KALYANI. I must have a talk with you in private.

KHIRI. Nothing can be more private than this. Only
      yourself and I. These are mere servants. Malati!

MALATI. Yes, Your Highness!

KHIRI. Is it possible to send them away?

MALATI. I shudder to think of it.

KALYANI. Then let me tell you briefly. Our Pathan
      King has forcibly robbed me of my lands.

KHIRI. You are not joking? Then those villages
      Gopalnagar, Kanaiganj and. . . .

KALYANI. They no longer belong to me.

KHIRI. That's interesting. Haven't you some cash left?

KALYANI. Nothing whatever.

KHIRI. How funny! That sapphire necklace and those
      wonderful diamonds and that chain of rubies,
      seven rows deep. . . .

KALYANI. They are all taken away.

KHIRI. Doesn't our scripture say that wealth is unstable

like a water drop on a lotus leaf? And your jewelled umbrella, and that throne with its canopy—I suppose they also have followed the rest.

KALYANI. Yes.

KHIRI. This is instructive. Our sages truly say that prosperity is like a beautiful dream that makes the awakening all the more dismal. But have they left you your palace?

KALYANI. The soldiers are in possession.

KHIRI. It does sound like a story—a Rani yesterday and today a beggar in the street. Malati!

MALATI. Yes, Your Highness!

KHIRI. What do you say?

MALATI. Those who grow too high must have their fall.

KALYANI. If I may have shelter here for a short time I can try to recover my lost fortune.

KHIRI. How unfortunate! My palace is crowded with
my servants—no space left where a needle can
be dropped. Of course I could leave you my
room and try to rough it in my country-house.

FIRST ATTENDANT. Absurd!

SECOND ATTENDANT. It will simply break our hearts.

KALYANI. I cannot dream of putting you to such
inconvenience. I take my leave.

KHIRI. Must you go so soon? By the by if you still have
some jewellry left, you may leave it with me for
permanent safe keeping.

KALYANI. Nothing has been saved.

KHIRI. How late it is. It gives me a headache if I am
made to talk too much I feel it already coming
on. [KALYANI *goes*.] See that my State chair and
footstool are carefully put back in the
storeroom. Malati!

MALATI. Yes, Your Highness!

KHIRI. What do you think of this?

MALATI. It makes one laugh to see the frog turning into
a tadpole again.

AN ATTENDANT. A woman craves your audience. Shall
I send her away.

KHIRI. No, no, call her in. I am in a delightful mood
today.

[*Enters the* WOMAN.]

THE WOMAN. I am in trouble.

KHIRI. You want to pass it on to others?

THE WOMAN. Robbers came to my room last night.

KHIRI. And you must take your revenge on me!

THE WOMAN. I ask for your pity.

KHIRI. Pity for what you have lost yourself and nothing
for what you ask me to lose?

THE WOMAN. If you must reject my prayer, tell me where
I may get it granted.

KHIRI. Kalyani is the proper person to suit you. My
men will go and show you her place.

THE WOMAN. Her place is well known to me,— I go
back to her! [*Revealing herself*] I am the Goddess
Lakshmi!

KHIRI. If you must leave me, do it in proper style.—
Malati, Malati, Tarini! Where are my maids?

[*Enters* KALYANI.]

KALYANI. Have you gone mad? It is still dark, and your
shouts bid fair to wake the whole
neighbourhood.

KHIRI. What ugly dreams I have had all night! It is a
new life to wake up from them. Stay a while,

let me take the dust of your feet. You are my Rani, and I am your servant for ever.

Autumn-Festival

CHARACTERS

Sanyasi, *Emperor Vijayaditya in disguise*

Thakurdada

Luckeswar

Upananda

Rajah

Boys

Minister, Courtiers, etc.

Scene. The forest near the river Vetasini.
LUCKESWAR *and* UPANANDA.

LUCKESWAR. Have you brought me the money
which is long overdue?

UPANANDA. My master died last night.

LUCKESWAR. Died! Absurd! That trick won't do.
What about the money?

UPANANDA. He hasn't left anything except the *vina*

which was his only means of paying off your debt.

LUCKESWAR. Only the *vina*! That's a consoling piece of news to bring to me.

UPANANDA. I haven't come to give you news. There was a time when I was a beggar in the street; he sheltered me and allowed me to share his food, which was scanty enough. I have come to offer my service till his debt is fully paid.

LUCKESWAR. Indeed! Now that he is no more you have come to share *my* food, which is not overabundant. I am not such an ass as to be taken in by you. However let me first know what you can do.

UPANANDA. I can copy manuscripts and illuminate them. Food I won't take in your house. I shall earn it and also pay off the debt.

LUCKESWAR. [*aside.*] The *vina* player was a big fool

and he has moulded this boy in his own pattern.

This vagabond is pining to take up some

voluntary burden to be crushed to death. For

some creatures this is the only natural death.—

Good, I agree. But you must pay me the money

on the third day of each month, otherwise—

UPANANDA. Otherwise what! Your threats are of

no use. In memory of my dear master I take

this up. But no threats for me, I warn you.

LUCKESWAR. Don't take offence, my child. You are

made of gold. Every inch of you; you are a

jewel. You know I have my god in the temple,

his worship depends upon my charity. If, owing

to my irregularity in your payment, I have to

curtail the temple expenses, the sin will be on

your head. [UPANANDA *moves away to another side of the forest.*] Who's that! It must be my own boy prowling about this place. I am sure the rogue is seeking for the place where I keep my treasure hidden. Simply out of fear of these prying noses I have to remove it from place to place.—Dhanapati, why on earth are you here?

DHANAPATI. If you give me leave, I can have my game here this morning with the other boys.

LUCKESWAR [*aside*]. I know their game. They have got scent of that big pearl which I hid near this spot. [*To* DHANAPATI] No, that won't do! Come at once to your multiplication table.

DHANAPATI. But, Sir, it is a beautiful day—

LUCKESWAR. What do you mean by the day being

beautiful! Come at once!

[*Drags him away.*]

[*Enter* BOYS *with* THAKURDADA.]

FIRST BOY. You belong to our party. Thakurdada!

SECOND BOY. No, to ours.

THAKURDADA. Children, I don't sell myself in
shares. I must remain undivided. Now for the
song.

[*They sing.*]

*Over the green and yellow ricefields sweeps
the shadows of the
autumn clouds followed by the swift-chasing
sun.
The bees forget to sip their honey; drunken
with light they
foolishly hover and hum.*

The ducks in the islands of the river clamour

in joy for nothing.

[*Enter another group of* BOYS.]

THIRD BOY. Was it fair? Why didn't you call us
when you came out?

THAKURDADA. It is your part to call me out. Don't
quarrel, finish the song.

[*They sing.*]

Let none go back home, brothers, this

morning, let none go to work,

Let us take the blue sky by storm and plunder

space as we run.

Laughter floats in the air like foam on the

flood.

Brothers, let us squander our morning in futile

songs.

FIRST BOY. Look there Thakurdada, a sanyasi is coming.

SECOND BOY. It's grand! We shall have a game with the sanyasi. We shall be his followers.

THIRD BOY. We shall follow him to the end of the earth and nobody will be able to find us out.

THAKURDADA. Hush, he has come.

THE BOYS [*shouting*]. Sanyasi Thakur! Sanyasi Thakur!

THAKURDADA. Stop that noise! The father will be angry.

FIRST BOY. Sanyasi Thakur, will you be angry with us?

SECOND BOY. We shall become your followers for this morning.

SANYASI. Excellent! When you have had your turn,
I shall be your followers. That will be splendid
fun!

THAKURDADA. My salutation. Who are you,
father?

SANYASI. I am a student.

THAKURDADA. Student!

SANYASI. I have come out to fling to the four winds
my books.

THAKURDADA. I understand. You want to be
lightened of your learning, to follow the path
of wisdom unburdened.

FIRST BOY. Thakurdada is wasting time with talk,
and our holiday will come to its close.

SANYASI. You are right, my boys. My holidays are
also near their end.

THE BOYS. Have you long holidays?

SANYASI. Oh! no, extremely short. My school-master

    is already after me.

FIRST BOY. You frighten us! Even *you* have school-

    masters?

SANYASI. What boy is that under the shade of that

    tree, merged in his manuscripts?

BOYS. He is Upananda.

FIRST BOY. Upananda, we are Sanyasi Thakur's

    followers, come and become our chief.

UPANANDA. Not to-day. I have my work.

SECOND BOY. No work. You *must* come!

UPANANDA. I must finish copying manuscripts.

THIRD BOY. Father, you ask him to come. He won't

    listen to us.

SANYASI. [*to* UPANANDA]. What work have you,

    my son? To-day is not meant for work.

UPANANDA. I know it is our holiday. But I have my debt to pay and I must work.

THAKURDADA. Upananda, your debt! To whom?

UPANANDA. My master has died, he is in debt to Luckeswar. I must pay it off.

THAKURDADA. Alas! that such a boy as you must pay your debts, and on such a day! The first breath of the autumn has sent a shiver through the white crest of flowering grass and the *shiuli* blossoms have offered their fragrance to the air, as if in the joy of reckless sacrifice, and it pains me to see that boy sitting in the midst of all this, toiling to pay his debts.

SANYASI. Why, this is as beautiful as all these flowers,—his paying his debts. He had made this morning glorious, sitting in its centre. Baba, you go on writing, let me watch you. Every line you finish brings you freedom, and thus you fill your holiday with truth. Give me one of your manuscripts and let me help you.

THAKURDADA. I have my spectacles with me, let me also sit down to this work.

FIRST BOY. We shall also write. This is great fun!

SECOND BOY. Yes, yes, let us try.

UPANANDA. But it will be such a great trouble to you, father.

SANYASI. That is why I join you. We shall take trouble for fun. What do you say to that, boys?

THE BOYS [*clapping hands*]. Yes, yes.

FIRST BOY. Give me one of the books.

SECOND BOY. And me also.

UPANANDA. But are you sure you can do it.

THE BOYS. O! Yes!

UPANANDA. You won't be tired?

SECOND BOY. Never.

UPANANDA. You will have to be very careful.

FIRST BOY. Try us.

UPANANDA. There must be no mistakes.

SECOND BOY. Not a bit.

SANYASI. Baba Upananda, what was your master's name?

UPANANDA. Surasen.

SANYASI. Surasen, the *vina* player?

UPANANDA. Yes, father. Was he known to you?

SANYASI. I came to this place with the one hope of hearing him.

UPANANDA. Had he such fame?

THAKURDADA. Was he such a master, that a sanyasi like yourself should have come all this way to hear him? Then we must have missed knowing him truly.

SANYASI. But the Rajah of this place?

THAKURDADA. The Rajah never even saw him. But where could you have heard him play?

SANYASI. I suppose you know that there is a Rajah whose name is Vijayaditya.

THAKURDADA. We may be very provincial, but surely you don't expect us not even to know him.

SANYASI. Very likely. Surasen played the *vina* in his court, where I was present. The Rajah tried hard to keep him permanently in his capital, but he failed.

THAKURDADA. What a pity that we did not honour him.

SANYASI. But that neglect has only made him all the greater. God has called him to His own court. Upananda, how did you come to know him?

UPANANDA. At my father's death I came to this town seeking shelter. It was at the end of July and the rain was pouring down in torrents. I was trying to find a corner in Lokanath temple, when the priest came and drove me out, expecting me to be of a low caste. My master was playing the *vina* in the temple. At once he came up and putting his arms round my neck asked me to come to his house. From that day he brought me up suffering calumny for my sake.

SANYASI. How did you learn illuminating manuscripts?

UPANANDA. At first I asked him to teach me to play the *vina*, so that I could earn something

and be useful to him. He said, 'Baba, this art is
not for filling one's stomach.' And so he taught
me how to use paints for copying books.

SANYASI. Though Surasen's *vina* is silent, I hear the
undying music of his life through you. My boy
go on with your writing.

THE BOYS [*starting up*]. There he comes. Lucki's
owl! We must run away.

[*They go.*]

[*Enters* LUCKESWAR.]

LUCKESWAR. Horror! Upananda is sitting exactly
on the spot where the pearl is hidden. I *was*
simple to think he was a fool seeking to pay off
other people's debts. He is cleverer than he
looked. He is after my pearl. I see he has
captured a sanyasi to help him. Upananda!

UPANANDA. What's the matter!

LUCKESWAR. Get up from that spot at once! What business have you to be sitting there!

UPANANDA. And what business have *you* to be shouting at me like that! Does this place belong to you?

LUCKESWAR. It is no concern of yours, if it does or does not.—You *are* cunning! The other day this fellow came to me, looking innocent as a babe whose mother's milk had hardly dried on his lips. And I believed him when he said that he came to pay his master's debts. Of course, it is in the King's statute also,—

UPANANDA. I sat down to my work here for that very purpose.

LUCKESWAR. That very purpose! How old am I do you think? Only born overnight?

SANYASI. But why do you suspect him and of what?

LUCKESWAR. As if you know nothing! False Sanyasi!

UPANANDA [*getting excited*]. Won't I just smash his teeth with this pestle of mine!

[LUCKESWAR *hides himself behind the* SANYASI.]

SANYASI. Don't be excited. Luckeswar knows human nature better than any of you here. Directly he sets his eyes upon me, I am caught,— a sanyasi false from his matted hair to his bare foot. I have passed through many countries and everywhere they believed in me, but Luckeswar is hard to deceive.

LUCKESWAR [*aside*]. I am afraid I am mistaken. It was rash on my part. He may curse me. I still have three boats on the sea. [*Taking the dust off sanyasi's feet.*] My salutation to you, father!

I did make a blunder. Thakurdada, you had better take our Sanyasi to our house. I'll give him some alms. But you go first; don't delay, I shall be there in a minute.

THAKURDADA. You are excessively kind. Do you think that father has come crossing hills and seas to accept a handful of rice from you?

SANYASI. Why not Thakurdada! Where that handful of rice is so very dear, I must claim it. Come Luckeswar!

LUCKESWAR. I shall follow you. Upananda, you get up first! Get up, I say, with your books and other nonsense.

UPANANDA. Very well, I get up. Then I cut off all connection with you for good.

LUCKESWAR. That will be a great relief to me. I was getting on splendidly before I had any connection with you.

UPANANDA. My debt is paid with this insult that I suffer from your hands.

LUCKESWAR. My God! Sepoys riding on horses are coming this way! I wonder if our Rajah also— I prefer Upananda to him. [*To* SANYASI] Father, by your holy feet I entreat you, sit on this spot, just on this spot; no, slightly to the left, slightly more. Yes, now it is all right. Sit firmly on this plot of grass. Let the Rajah come or the Emperor, don't you budge an inch. If you keep my words, I'll satisfy you later on.

THAKURDADA. What is the matter with Luckeswar? Has he gone mad?

LUCKESWAR. Father, the very sight of me suggests money to my Rajah. My enemies have falsely informed him that I keep my treasure hidden underground. Since this report, our Rajah has been digging an enormous number of wells in this kingdom. When asked for reasons, he said it was to remove the scarcity of water from this land. And now I can't sleep at nights because of the fear that a sudden fit of his generosity might lead him to remove the water scarcity from the floor of my own dwelling.

[*Enters the King's* MESSENGER.]

MESSENGER. Father, my salutation! You are Apurva-Ananda?

SANYASI. Some people know me by that name.

MESSENGER. The rumour is abroad of your extraordinary powers. Our Rajah is desirous of seeing you.

SANYASI. He will see me whenever he sets his eyes
on me.

MESSENGER. If you would kindly—

SANYASI. I have given my word to somebody that I
shall remain immovable in this place.

MESSENGER. The King's garden is close by.

SANYASI. All the less trouble for him to come.

MESSENGER. I shall make known to him your wishes.

[*Goes.*]

THAKURDADA. Since an irruption of Rajahs is
apprehended, I take my leave.

SANYASI. Do you gather my scattered friends
together and keep them ready for me.

THAKURDADA. Let disasters come in the shape of
Kings or of anarchy, I firmly hold by you.

[*Goes.*]

[*Enters* LUCKESWAR.]

LUCKESWAR. I have overheard all. You are the famous Apurva-Ananda! I ask your pardon for the liberties I have taken.

SANYASI. I readily pardon you for your calling me a sham sanyasi.

LUCKESWAR. But father, mere pardon does not cost much. You cannot dismiss Luckeswar with that. I must have a boon,—quite a substantial one.

SANYASI. What boon do you ask?

LUCKESWAR. I must confess to you, father, that I have piled up a little money for myself, though not quite to the measure of what people imagine. But the amount does not satisfy me. Tell me the secret of some treasure, which may lead me to the end of my wanderings.

SANYASI. I am also seeking for this.

LUCKESWAR. I can't believe it.

SANYASI. Yes, it is true.

LUCKESWAR. Then you are wider awake than we are.

SANYASI. Certainly.

LUCKESWAR. [*whispering*]. Have you got on the track?

SANYASI. Otherwise I shouldn't be roving about like this.

LUCKESWAR. [*touching his feet*]. Do make it a little plain to me. I swear I shall keep it secret from everybody else.

SANYASI. Then listen. I am on the quest of the golden lotus on which Lakshmi keeps her feet.

LUCKESWAR. How bold! This takes my breath away. But, do you think you can find it unaided? It

means expense. Do one thing, let us go shares
in it.

SANYASI. In that case you will have to be a sanyasi,
never touching gold for a long time.

LUCKESWAR. That is hard.

SANYASI. You can only prosper in this business if
you give up all others.

LUCKESWAR. That sounds very much like
bankruptcy. But all the same I *do* believe in
you—which astounds even myself. There
comes our Rajah! Let me hide behind this tree.

[*Hides himself.*]

[*Enters the* RAJAH.]

RAJAH. My salutation!

SANYASI. Victory to you! What is your desire?

RAJAH. Surely you can divine it already. My desire

is to rule over a kingdom which is supreme.

SANYASI. Then begin by giving up what is small.

RAJAH. The overlordship of Vijayaditya has become

intolerable to me.

SANYASI. To tell you the truth he is growing too

much even for me.

RAJAH. Is that so?

SANYASI. Yes. All my practices are to bring him

under control.

RAJAH. Is that why you have become a sanyasi?

SANYASI. Yes.

RAJAH. Do you think your charms will be potent

enough to bring you success?

SANYASI. It is not impossible.

RAJAH. In that case do not forget me.

SANYASI. I shall bring him to your court.

RAJAH. Yes, his pride must be brought low.

SANYASI. That will do him good.

RAJAH. With your leave I take my departure.

[*Goes.*]

[*Returning*] Father, I am sure you know Vijayaditya personally—is he as great as the people make him out to be?

SANYASI. He is like an ordinary person,—it is his dress which gives him a false distinction.

RAJAH. Just what I thought. Quite an ordinary person!

SANYASI. I want to convince him that he is very much so. I must free his mind from the notion that he is a different creature from others.

Rajah. Yes, yes, let him feel it. Fools puff him up and he believes them, being the greatest of their kind. Pull down his conceit to the dust.

SANYASI. I am engaged in that difficult task.

[*The* RAJAH *goes.*]

[*Enters* UPANANDA.]

UPANANDA. Father, the burden is not yet off my
mind.

SANYASI. What is it that troubles you, my son?

UPANANDA. In my anger, at the insult offered to
me, I thought I was right in disowning my debt
to him. Therefore I went back home. But just
as I was dusting my master's *vina* its strings
struck up a chord and it sent a thrill through
my heart. I felt that I must do something super-
human for my master. If I can lay down my life
to pay his debts for him, this beautiful day of
October will then have its full due from me.

SANYASI. Baba, what you say is true.

UPANANDA. Father, you have seen many countries, do you know of any great man who is likely to buy a boy like me for a thousand *kahan*? That is all that I need for the debt.

SANYASI. What do you say to trying Vijayaditya, who used to be so fond of your master?

UPANANDA. Vijayaditya? But he is our emperor.

SANYASI. Is that so?

UPANANDA. Don't you know that?

SANYASI. But what if he *is* your emperor?

UPANANDA. Do you think he will care to pay any price for a boy like myself?

SANYASI. I can assure you, that he will be ashamed of his full treasury, if he does not pay your debt.

UPANANDA. Is that possible, father?

SANYASI. Do you think in God's world Luckeswar

     is the only possibility?

UPANANDA. But I must not idly wait for chances.

     In the meanwhile, let me go on with my work

     and pay off in small parts what I owe.

SANYASI. Yes, my boy, take up your burden.

UPANANDA. I feel ever so much stronger, for having

     known you. Now I take my leave.

[*Goes.*]

[*Enters* LUCKESWAR.]

LUCKESWAR. I give it up. It is not in my power to

     be your follower. With an infinite struggle I

     have earned what I have done. To leave all

     that, at your bidding, and then to repent of my

     rashness till the end of my days, would be worse

     than madness: it would be so awfully unlike

myself. Now then, father, you must move from your seat.

SANYASI· [*rising*]. Then I have got my release from you?

LUCKESWAR. [*taking out a jewel case from under some turf and dry leaves*]. For this tiny little thing I have been haunting this place, like a ghost from the morning. You are the first human being to whom I have shown this. [*Holding it up to him and then hastily withdrawing it*] No, impossible! I fully trust you, yet I have not the power to put it into your hands even for a moment. Merely holding it in the light makes my heart palpitate. Can you tell me, father, what kind of man is Vijayaditya? If I try to sell it to him, are you sure he won't take it away by force? Can you trust him?

SANYASI. Not always.

LUCKESWAR. Well, that does not sound promising. I suspect, after all, this will lie underground, and after my death nobody will be able to find it.

SANYASI. Neither Kings nor Emperors, but the dust will claim it as its final tribute.

LUCKESWAR. Let it; that does not trouble me. But my anxiety is lest some one should discover it, when I am no more....However, father, I shall never forget about that golden lotus. I feel sure you will get it some day; but all the same I cannot be your follower.

[*Goes.*]

[*Enters* THAKURDADA.]

SANYASI. After long days I have learnt one thing at last, and that I must tell you.

THAKURDADA. Father, you are very kind to me.

SANYASI. I know why this world is so beautiful,— simply because it is ever paying back its debt. The ricefield has done its utmost to earn its fulfilment and the Betasini River is what it is because it keeps nothing back.

THAKURDADA. I understand, father. There is One Who has given Himself in creation in his abundance of joy. And Creation is every moment working to repay the gift, and this perpetual sacrifice is blossoming everywhere in beauty and life.

SANYASI. Wherever there is sluggishness, there accumulates debt, and there it is ugly.

THAKURDADA. Because where there is a lacking

in the gift, the harmony is broken in the eternal

rhythm of the payment and repayment.

[*Enters* LUCKESWAR.]

LUCKESWAR. What are you two people conspiring

about?

SANYASI. About that golden lotus.

LUCKESWAR. Have you already given away your

secret to Thakurdada? You hope to be

successful when you do your business in such

a manner? But is Thakurdada the proper man

to help you? How much capital has he, do you

think?

SANYASI. You don't know the secret. He has quite

a big amount, though he does not show it.

LUCKESWAR. [*slapping* THAKURDADA *on the shoulder*]. You are deep. I never thought of that. And yet people only suspect *me* and not you, not even the Rajah himself....Father, I can't bear Thakurdada to steal a march on me. Let all three of us join in this business. Look there, a crowd of people is coming this way. They must have got news that a Swami is here. Father, they will wear out your feet upto the knees taking the dust of them. But I warn you, father, you are too simple. Don't take anybody else into your confidence....But, Thakurdada, you must know business is not mere child's play. The chances of loss are eleven to one— keep that in mind. I give it up. But no, I must take time to decide.

[*Goes.*]

[Enter VILLAGERS.]

FIRST VILLAGER. Where is the sanyasi they talked about?

SECOND VILLAGER. Is this the man?

THIRD VILLAGER. He looks like a fraud. Where is the real one.

SANYASI. A real one is difficult to find. I am playing at sanyasi to amuse boys.

FIRST VILLAGER. But we are not boys.

SANYASI. I know the distinction.

SECOND VILLAGER. Then why did someone say, that some swami is somewhere about?

FIRST VILLAGER. But your appearance is good. Have you learnt some charms?

SANYASI. I am willing to learn. But who is to teach me?

SECOND VILLAGER. There is a proper man. He lives in Bhairabpur. He has control over some spirits, and there is no doubt of that. Only the other day a boy was about to die. And what do you think this man did? He simply let the boy's life-spark fly into the inside of a panther. You won't believe it, but I can assure you, that panther is still alive, though the boy died. You may laugh, but my own brother-in-law has seen the panther with his own eyes. If anybody tries to injure it, the father rushes at him with his big stick. The man is quite ruining himself by offering kids twice a day to this beast. If you must learn charms, this is the man for you.

THIRD VILLAGER. What is the use of wasting time? Didn't I tell you in the beginning, that I didn't believe a word about this sanyasi. There are

very few people in these days who have magic
powers.

SECOND VILLAGER. That is true. But I was told by
Kalu's mother that her nephew knew a Sanyasi
who overturned his pipe of ganja and there
came out a skull and a full pot of liquor.

THIRD VILLAGER. But did he see it with his own
eyes?

SECOND VILLAGER. Yes, with his very own eyes.

[*They go.*]

[*Enters* LUCKESWAR.]

LUCKESWAR. I can't stand this. You must take away
your charm from me. My accounts are all
getting wrong. My head is in a muddle. Now I
feel quite reckless about that golden lotus, and
now it seems pure foolishness. Now I am afraid

Thakurdada will win, and now I say to myself let Thakurdada go to the dogs. But this doesn't seem right. It is sorcery for the purpose of kidnapping. No, no, that will never do with me. What is there to smile about? I am pretty tough, and you shall never have *me* for your disciple.

[*Enter* BOYS.]

FIRST BOY. We are ready for the autumn festival. What must we do?

SANYASI. We must begin with a song.

[*Sings.*]

The breeze has touched the white sails, the boat
revels in the beauty of its dancing speed.
It sings of the treasure of the distant shore, it lures
my heart to the voyage of the perilous quest.

The captain stands at his helm with the sun shining

on his face and the rain-clouds looming behind.

My heart aches to know how to sing to him of

tears

and smiles made one in joy.

SANYASI. Now you have seen the face of the autumn.

FIRST BOY. But where is it, father?

SANYASI. Don't you see those white clouds sailing

on?

SECOND BOY. Yes, yes.

THIRD BOY. Yes, I can see them.

SANYASI. The sky fills up.

FIRST BOY. With what?

SANYASI. With light. And don't you feel the touch

of the dew in the air?

SECOND BOY. Yes.

SANYASI. Only look at that Betasini River—what
headlong rush to spend herself. And see the
shiver in the young shoots of rice Thakurdada,
let the boys sing the welcome song of the
autumn and go round the forests and hills
yonder.

[THAKURDADA *sings and the* BOYS *join him.*]

*I have spread my heart in the sky and found
your touch in my dreams*
*Take away that veil from your face, let me see
your eyes.*
*There rings your welcome at the doors of the
forest fairies;*
*your anklet bells sound
in all my thoughts*

filling my work with music.

[The Boys *go out singing.*]

[*Enters* LUCKESWAR.]

THAKURDADA. Hallo! Our Luckeswar in a sanyasi's garb!

LUCKESWAR. I have become your disciple at last father. Here is my pearl-case, and here are the jewel caskets. Take care of them.

SANYASI. Why has this sudden change come over you?

LUCKESWAR. The Emperor Vijayaditya's army is marching towards this town. Nobody will dare touch you, so you are the safest man to whom I can entrust my treasure.—I am your devoted follower,—protect me!

[*Enters the* RAJAH]

RAJAH. Father!

SANYASI. Sit down. You seem to be out of breath.
Rest a while.

RAJAH. No time for rest. I am informed that
Vijayaditya is almost upon us. His flag has been
seen.

SANYASI. Very likely. He must be feeling eager to
acquire new dominions.

RAJAH. What do you say? New dominions?

SANYASI. Why do you take offence at it, my son?
You also had a similar idea.

RAJAH. Oh! no, that was quite different. But
whatever that might be, I ask for your
protection. Some mischief-makers must have
carried tales to him. Please tell him, they are

all lies. Am I mad, that I should want to be the Emperor? Have I got the power.

SANYASI. Thakurdada!

THAKURDADA. Yes, my master!

SANYASI. Simply with this rag upon my back and a few boys as my followers, I was fully successful in making this day glorious. But look at this wretched man,—this emperor,—he has power only to ruin it.

RAJAH. Hush! Somebody may overhear you!

SANYASI. I must fight it out with that—

RAJAH. I won't allow it. You are becoming dangerous. Can't you keep your sentiments to yourself?

SANYASI. But I already had a discussion about this with you, haven't I?

RAJAH. What an awful man you are! Luckeswar, why are you here? Leave this place at once.

LUCKESWAR. Sire, I can tell you, it is not for the
pure pleasure of your presence that I am here.
I should be only too glad to get away, but I am
fixed to this spot. I have not the power to
move.

[*Enter* VIJAYADITYA'S MINISTER *and courtiers.*]

MINISTER. Victory to the Emperor Vijayaditya!
[*They all bow.*]

RAJAH. Stop that stupid jest! I am not Vijayaditya.
I am his most unworthy servant—Somapal.
MINISTER [*to the* SANYASI]. Sire, the time has
come for you to come back to your capital.
THAKURDADA. My master, is this a dream?
SANYASI. Whether your dream or theirs is true who
can tell.

THAKURDADA. Then—

SANYASI. Yes, these people happen to know me as
Vijayaditya.

THAKURDADA. But this new situation has made
things critical for me.

LUCKESWAR. And for me also. I surrendered myself
to the sanyasi in order to be saved from the
Emperor. But I do not know in whose hands I
am now.

RAJAH. Sire, did you come to try me?

SANYASI. And also myself.

RAJAH. What is to be my punishment?

SANYASI. To leave you to your memory.

[*Enters* UPANANDA.]

UPANANDA. Who are these people? Oh! here is
the Rajah. [*About to leave.*]

SANYASI. Upananda, do not go! Tell me what you

had come to say.

UPANANDA. I came to tell you that I had earned this three *Kahans* by my days' work.

SANYASI. Give them to me. They are too valuable to go for clearing Luckeswar's debt. I take these for myself.

UPANANDA. Must you take these, father?

SANYASI. Yes, I must. Do you think I have mastered my greed, because I have become a sanyasi? These tempt me beyond anything else.

LUCKESWAR. This sounds ominous! I am undone!

SANYASI. Where is my treasurer?

TREASURER. Here I am.

SANYASI. Let this man have a thousand *Kahan* from my treasury.

UPANANDA. Then does he buy me?

SANYASI. You are mine. [*To the* MINISTER] You

were troubled, because no son had been born to my house. But I have earned my son, by my merit, and here he is.

LUCKESWAR. How unlucky for me that I am too old for such adoption!

SANYASI. Luckeswar!

LUCKESWAR. Command me!

SANYASI. I have protected your jewels from the grasp of Vijayaditya. Now they are given back to you.

LUCKESWAR. If the Maharajah had given them back in secret, I could feel secure. Who is to save them now?

SANYASI. That is my business. But Luckeswar, something is due to me from you.

LUCKESWAR [*aside*]. Curse me! I knew it would come at last.

SANYASI. Thakurdada is witness to my claim.

LUCKESWAR [*aside*]. There will be no lack of false
    witnesses for him now.

SANYASI. You wanted to give me alms. You owe me
    a handful of rice. Do you think you will be able
    to fill an Emperor's hand?

LUCKESWAR. But, Sire, it was a sanyasi's hand which
    gave me courage to propose what I did.

SANYASI. Then I free you from your promise.

LUCKESWAR. With the Maharajah's leave I take
    my departure. Everybody's eyes seem to be
    turned upon these caskets.

[*He goes.*]

[*Enter the* BOYS.]

Boys [*shouting*]. Sanyasi Thakur! [*They suddenly stop
    and are about to run away.*]

THAKURDADA. Boys, do not go.

SANYASI. Rajah, leave me.

[RAJAH *goes.*]

[*To his courtiers*] And you also.

Now back to our festival.

[*They go.*]

notes

_____

_____

_____

_____

_____

_____

_____

_____

_____

_____

_____

_____

_____

_____

_____

_____